Our Favorite
Speedy Slow-Cooker
Recipes

Copyright 2022, Gooseberry Patch
Previously published under ISBN 978-1-93628-375-0
Cover: Slow-Cooker Roast for Tacos (page 29)

How to Use Your Slow Cooker

 For best results, fill your slow cooker from 1/2 to 3/4 full. Food will be oh-so tasty and tender.

 Speed up a slow-cooker recipe to suit your own schedule... 2 to 2-1/2 hours on low equals one hour on high.

If a slow-cooker recipe calls for a spritz of non-stick vegetable spray to the inside crock, try placing a disposable slow-cooker liner inside instead...cleaning up will be a breeze!

 Don't peek! Cooking time can increase by 15 to 20 minutes each time the lid is lifted!

 Slow cookers come in all sizes, so why not have a couple on hand? A large slow cooker is ideal for family-size roasts, while a smaller one is just right for dips and fondue.

Ground meats should be browned and drained before using in a slow-cooker recipe...this eliminates grease!

 Slice & dice meats and veggies ahead of time and refrigerate in separate plastic zipping bags. In the morning, toss everything into the slow cooker!

 Remember to put veggies in the slow cooker first...they take longer to cook than the meat or poultry.

 Thaw or rinse frozen veggies before placing them in your slow cooker. Otherwise, they'll keep your dish from heating up as quickly as possible.

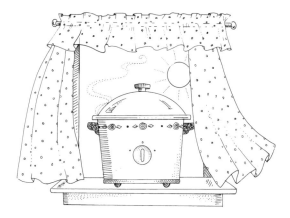

For a speedy breakfast, keep all the ingredients in
one spot for favorite slow-cooker recipes.

Tasty Hashbrown Casserole

Makes 6 servings

32-oz. pkg. frozen shredded
   hashbrowns, thawed
1 onion, diced
16-oz. jar pasteurized process
   cheese sauce, warmed

16-oz. container French
   onion dip
1/2 c. butter, melted

Combine all ingredients together; pour into a slow cooker. Cover and cook on low setting for 5 hours. Uncover; let stand for 10 minutes before serving.

Ham is so versatile...friends can enjoy it as the main dish,
or sliced very thin and arranged on split biscuits or bagels,
it's an easy-to-eat sandwich.

Rise & Shine Ham

Serves 8 to 10

6 to 8-lb. picnic ham, trimmed
64-oz. bottle apple juice
1 c. brown sugar, packed

3 to 4 T. apple jelly
2 T. maple syrup

Trim skin and excess fat from ham. Place onto a cutting board. With a sharp knife, score ham in a diamond pattern, making cuts about one to 1-1/2 inches apart. Place ham into slow cooker flat-side down. Pour in enough apple juice to cover. Cover and cook on low setting for 6 hours. Transfer to a lightly greased baking sheet; set aside. Mix brown sugar, apple jelly and maple syrup together in a bowl; spread onto ham. Bake at 375 degrees for 30 to 40 minutes, until topping is bubbling and glazed.

When cooking with apples, look for apples with characteristics similar to the recipe. Granny Smith apples are versatile as they hold their shape while baking and have a delicious sweet-tart flavor.

Mamaw's Breakfast Cobbler

Serves 4

2 c. tart apples, peeled, cored
    and sliced
2 c. granola cereal

1 t. cinnamon
1/4 c. honey
2 T. butter, melted

Combine apples, cereal and cinnamon in a lightly greased slow cooker and mix well. Stir together honey and butter; drizzle over apple mixture. Blend gently. Cover and cook on low setting for 8 hours, or until apples are tender.

Taking a filled slow cooker to a party can be tricky. To keep the lid secure, slip a large rubber band under one handle, twist it around the knob on the lid and wrap under the other handle.

Aunt Becky's Smoky Sausages

Makes 8 servings

14-oz. pkg. mini smoked
    sausages
28-oz. bottle barbecue sauce
1-1/4 c. water

3 T. Worcestershire sauce
2 T. steak sauce
1/2 t. pepper

Combine all ingredients in a slow cooker; mix well. Cover and cook
on low setting for 6 to 8 hours.

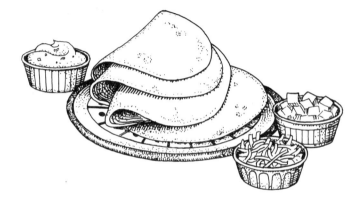

To warm tortillas, stack them between moistened paper towels
and microwave on high setting for 20 to 30 seconds...easy!

Slow-Cooker Chicken Tacolados

Serves 6 to 8

5 boneless, skinless
   chicken thighs
2 boneless, skinless
   chicken breasts
10-oz. can green enchilada
   sauce

10-3/4 oz. can cream of
   chicken soup
12 to 15 10-inch flour tortillas,
   warmed
Garnish: salsa

Arrange chicken pieces in a slow cooker; set aside. Combine sauce and soup in a bowl; blend well and pour over chicken. Cover and cook on low setting for 8 hours, or on high setting for 4 hours. When chicken is tender, shred with 2 forks. Serve on warmed tortillas; garnish as desired.

Slow cookers are perfect party helpers! Just plug them in and they'll keep dips bubbly, hot and yummy with no effort at all.

Our Favorite Fondue

Makes 3-1/2 cups

1-1/2 to 2 c. milk
2 8-oz. pkgs. cream cheese,
    softened

1-1/2 c. grated Parmesan cheese
1/2 t. garlic salt
1 loaf French bread, cubed

In a large saucepan, cook and stir milk and cream cheese over low heat until cream cheese is melted. Stir in Parmesan cheese and garlic salt; cook and stir until heated through. Transfer to a slow cooker; keep warm. Serve with bread cubes.

Show your hometown spirit...cheer on the high school
football team with a Friday neighborhood block party. Invite
neighbors to bring along their favorite appetizer to share
and don't forget to wear school colors!

Spicy Tailgate Dip

Serves 16 to 20

1 lb. ground pork sausage,
    browned and drained
2 8-oz. pkgs. cream
    cheese, cubed

10-oz. can tomatoes with chiles
corn chips

Combine all ingredients except chips in slow cooker. Cover and cook
on low setting for one to 2 hours, until heated through and cream
cheese is melted. Serve with corn chips.

No one can resist fresh salsa and chips! Pile blue and yellow
tortilla chips in a colorful bowl, placed in the middle of a large
plate or platter. Add a bowl of tangy homemade
salsa...what could be faster?

Summertime Salsa

Makes about 2 cups

10 plum tomatoes, cored
2 cloves garlic
1 onion, cut into wedges

2 jalapeño peppers, seeded
1/4 c. fresh cilantro
Optional: 1/2 t. salt

Cut a small slit in 2 tomatoes; insert a garlic clove into each. Place all tomatoes, onion and peppers in a slow cooker. Cover and cook on high setting for 2-1/2 to 3 hours, or until vegetables are tender; cool. Combine tomato mixture, cilantro and salt, if using, in a blender or food processor. Process until smooth. Serve immediately or refrigerate until ready to serve.

It's easy to convert your favorite stew recipe from stovetop to slow cooker. If it usually simmers 35 to 45 minutes, that equals 6 to 8 hours on low or 3 to 4 hours on high.

Montana Wild Rice Beef Stew

Serves 6

4 c. sliced mushrooms
3 carrots, peeled and sliced
    1/2-inch thick
6-oz. pkg. long-grain and
    wild rice

1 lb. beef sirloin, cubed
5 c. beef broth

Combine mushrooms, carrots and rice mix with seasoning packet in a slow cooker. Top with beef; pour broth over top. Cover and cook on low setting for 8 to 10 hours.

For flavorful, fast-fix bread to serve with soups, simply brush Italian bread slices with butter. Sprinkle on garlic & herb seasoning blend and broil until golden.

Pig-in-a-Poke Ham Soup

Makes 10 servings

4 14-1/2 oz. cans green beans   1 onion, sliced
1 meaty ham bone   pepper to taste
4 potatoes, peeled and quartered

In a slow cooker, combine undrained green beans and remaining
ingredients. Cover and cook on high setting for one hour. Reduce to
low setting; cover and cook for 6 to 7 hours, until the meat falls off
the bone. Remove ham bone; dice meat and return to slow cooker.

Chowders and cream soups are perfect comfort foods.
Make them extra creamy and rich tasting...simply replace milk
or water in the recipe with an equal amount of evaporated milk.

Game-Day Corn Chowder

Serves 6

1 lb. smoked pork sausage
3 c. frozen hashbrowns with
    onions and peppers
2 carrots, peeled and chopped
15-oz. can creamed corn

10-3/4 oz. can cream of
    mushroom with roasted
    garlic soup
2 c. water

Brown sausage in a skillet over medium heat; drain and cut into
bite-size pieces. Place sausage in a slow cooker; top with hashbrowns
and carrots. In a medium bowl, combine corn, soup and water; mix
until blended. Pour over sausage mixture. Cover and cook on low
setting for 8 to 10 hours.

Oh-so clever! Alongside each slow cooker, use Scrabble® game pieces to spell out soup names. Guests will know just what's inside and it's a fun twist on the traditional table tent.

Pasta Fagioli Soup

Makes 4 servings

1 lb. ground beef, browned
    and drained
18.8-oz. can minestrone soup

10-oz. can tomatoes with chiles
16-oz. can pinto or kidney
    beans, drained and rinsed

Combine all ingredients in a slow cooker. Cover and cook on low setting for 2 to 3 hours.

Fill a muffin tin with fixings like sliced black olives, chopped green onion and diced avocado...everyone can top their own tacos to their liking.

Slow-Cooker Roast for Tacos   *Makes about 10 cups*

4 to 5-lb. beef chuck roast
1 T. chili powder
1 t. ground cumin
1 t. onion powder

1 t. garlic powder
2 14-1/2 oz. cans Mexican-
      style stewed tomatoes
taco shells

Place roast in a large slow cooker; sprinkle with spices. Add tomatoes
with juice around the roast. Cover and cook on low setting for 8 to
10 hours. Using 2 forks, shred roast and return to slow cooker. Spoon
into taco shells.

Toast buns slightly before adding shredded or sliced meat...
it only takes a minute and makes such a tasty difference.

French Dip Au Jus

Makes 6 to 8 sandwiches

3 to 4-lb. beef rump roast
1 c. soy sauce

1-1/2 oz. pkg. onion soup mix
6 to 8 hoagie buns, split

Place roast in a slow cooker; pour soy sauce over top. Sprinkle soup mix over roast; fill slow cooker with enough water to cover roast. Cover and cook on low setting for 10 to 12 hours. Slice or shred meat; serve on rolls. Pour juices from slow cooker into small bowls for dipping.

Feeding a crowd is a breeze with a slow cooker. Fill it
with shredded meat, burgers or meatballs, set out
bakery-fresh rolls, chips and coleslaw...and you're
ready to just let guests help themselves!

Zippy Shredded Pork

Makes 6 servings

2 to 3-lb. boneless pork
    loin roast
salt and pepper to taste
16-oz. jar salsa

Optional: hot pepper sauce,
    chopped green chiles
6 hard rolls, split

Place roast in a slow cooker; sprinkle with salt and pepper. Pour salsa over roast; add hot sauce or chiles for extra heat, if desired. Cover and cook on low setting for 8 to 10 hours, until meat shreds easily. Stir meat to shred completely and serve on rolls.

Dinner Menu

Appetizers
olives, bread sticks, and salsa.

Soup & Salad
Chinese slaw.   house salad

Main
Royal Crown Beef Roast

Sides
mini-wrapped potatoes & curly fries

Dessert & Coffee
New York Style Cheesecake & Cappuccino

Keep the week's running menu at a glance. Tack extra-wide rick rack to a bulletin board and just slip your grocery list underneath.

Made-Rights

Makes 20 to 24 sandwiches

4 lbs. ground beef
3 c. water
1 c. cola

1/2 c. mustard
1 c. catsup
20 to 24 sandwich buns, split

Combine ground beef, water and cola in a slow cooker. With a potato masher, break the beef apart. Cover and cook on low setting for 8 to 10 hours. After beef is thoroughly cooked, mash again; drain well. Stir in mustard and catsup; serve on sandwich buns.

Pick up a stack of retro-style plastic burger baskets.
Lined with crisp paper napkins, they're still such fun
for serving hot dogs, burgers and fries.

Cheesy Chili Dogs

Makes 10 servings

1 lb. hot dogs
2 15-oz. cans chili, with or
    without beans
10-3/4 oz. can Cheddar
    cheese soup
4-oz. can chopped green chiles

10 hot dog buns, split
Garnish: chopped onion,
    shredded Cheddar cheese,
    crushed chili-cheese
    corn chips

Place hot dogs in a slow cooker. Combine chili, soup and chiles; pour over hot dogs. Cover and cook on low setting for 3 to 3-1/2 hours. Serve hot dogs in buns; top with hot chili mixture and garnish as desired.

To make clean-up a breeze, lightly spray the inside of a
slow cooker with non-stick vegetable spray, then
add recipe ingredients. What a time-saver!

Carolina Chicken Pitas

Makes 4 sandwiches

1 onion, chopped
1 lb. boneless, skinless
   chicken thighs
1 t. lemon-pepper seasoning

1/2 t. dried oregano
1/2 c. plain yogurt
4 pita bread rounds, halved
   and split

Combine all ingredients except yogurt and pitas in a slow cooker; mix well. Cover and cook on low setting for 6 to 8 hours. Just before serving, remove chicken from slow cooker and shred with 2 forks. Return shredded chicken back to slow cooker; stir in yogurt. Spoon into pita bread.

Need a tablecloth fast? Simply toss a quilt on the table!

Carol's Cheesy Potato Bake

Makes 10 to 12 servings

32-oz. pkg. frozen French fries
2 10-3/4 oz. cans cream of
    chicken soup

1 lb. smoked pork sausage, cut
    into bite-size pieces
2 c. shredded Cheddar cheese

Spray a slow cooker with non-stick vegetable spray. Layer ingredients in the following order: half of French fries, one can of soup, half of sausage and half of cheese. Repeat layers. Cover and cook on high setting for 4 hours. Stir just before serving.

When slow cooking at higher altitudes, recipes tend to take a bit longer. Add an extra 30 minutes of cooking time to each hour in a recipe.

Creamy Dijon Potatoes

Serves 4 to 6

6 potatoes, peeled and sliced
10-3/4 oz. can cream of
    chicken soup
3 T. Dijon mustard

1 onion, sliced
1 green pepper, sliced
Optional: 1 t. cayenne pepper

Place potatoes in a slow cooker. Combine soup and mustard; spread over potatoes. Top with onion and green pepper. Sprinkle with cayenne pepper, if desired. Cover and cook on low setting for 6 to 8 hours.

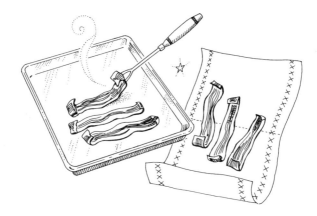

A quick, no-mess way to cook bacon. Arrange slices on a
broiler pan and place 3 to 4 inches under the broiler. Broil for
one to 2 minutes on each side, depending on how crispy
you like your bacon.

Potato Lady Potatoes

Makes 12 to 15 servings

4 15-oz. cans sliced potatoes,
   drained
2 10-3/4 oz. cans cream of
   celery soup

16-oz. container sour cream
1/2 lb. bacon, crisply cooked
   and crumbled
1 bunch green onions, sliced

Place potatoes in a slow cooker. Combine all remaining ingredients;
add to potatoes and mix well. Cover and cook on low setting for 2 to
3 hours, stirring occasionally.

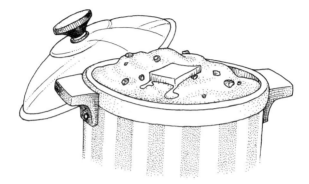

Try a delicious secret the next time you make the
potatoes...substitute equal parts chicken broth and cream
for the milk in any favorite recipe.

Garlic Smashed Potatoes

Makes 4 to 6 servings

3 lbs. redskin potatoes, halved
   or quartered
4 cloves garlic, minced
2 T. olive oil
1 t. salt

1/2 c. water
1/2 c. cream cheese with chives
   and onions
1/4 to 1/2 c. milk

Place potatoes in a slow cooker. Add garlic, oil, salt and water; mix well to coat potatoes. Cover and cook on high setting for 3-1/2 to 4-1/2 hours, until potatoes are tender. Mash potatoes with a potato masher or fork. Stir in cream cheese until well blended; add enough milk for soft consistency. Serve immediately, or keep warm in slow cooker on low setting for up to 2 hours.

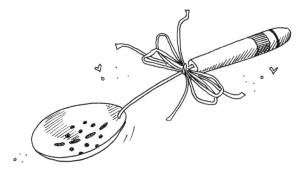

Besides the ease of letting a slow cooker do all the work,
another advantage is that it uses very little electricity.
On average, it costs just 21 cents to operate a slow cooker
for a total of 10 hours!

Zesty Ranch Potatoes

Makes 6 to 8 servings

6 potatoes, peeled and quartered
1/2 c. cream cheese, softened
1/4 c. margarine, softened
1-oz. pkg. ranch salad
    dressing mix
1 t. dried parsley

Cover potatoes with water in a saucepan. Bring to a boil over medium-high heat. Cook until potatoes are tender, about 15 to 20 minutes. Drain; mash potatoes and mix with remaining ingredients. Spoon into a slow cooker. Cover and cook on low setting for 2 to 4 hours.

When it comes to carving squash, try using the knife
that comes in a pumpkin carving kit...its little size is
just right for slicing squash!

Sausage-Stuffed Squash

Makes 4 servings

14-oz. pkg. smoked pork
   sausage, diced
1/3 c. dark brown sugar, packed
1 T. butter-flavored sprinkles

1/4 t. dried sage
2 acorn squash, halved
   and seeded
1 c. water

Mix sausage, brown sugar, sprinkles and sage together; toss to coat
sausage with seasonings. Fill squash halves heaping full with
sausage mixture; wrap each stuffed half with aluminum foil. Pour
water into a slow cooker; place wrapped squash halves in slow
cooker, stacking if necessary. Cover and cook on low setting for 6 to
8 hours.

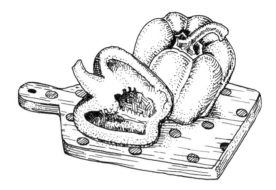

A speedy side...stir-fry frozen green beans
until crisp-tender, and toss with a jar
of roasted red pepppers.

Pennsylvania Stuffed Peppers

Serves 6

1-1/2 lbs. ground beef
1 egg, beaten
1 c. orzo pasta or instant
    rice, uncooked
garlic salt and pepper to taste

6 green, yellow or red peppers,
    tops removed
2 10-3/4 oz. cans tomato soup
2-1/2 c. water

Mix beef, egg, uncooked orzo or rice and seasonings in a bowl. Stuff peppers lightly with mixture. If any extra beef mixture remains, form into small meatballs. In a slow cooker, blend together soup and water. Arrange stuffed peppers in slow cooker; replace tops on peppers for a nice touch. Place meatballs around peppers. Lightly spoon some of soup mixture onto tops of peppers. Cover and cook on low setting for 8 to 10 hours.

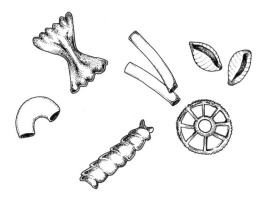

Try using a different shape of pasta next time you make
macaroni & cheese. Wagon wheels, seashells and bow ties
all hold cheese sauce well…they're fun for kids too!

Macaroni & Cheese

Makes 12 to 16 servings

1/2 c. butter
1/2 c. all-purpose flour
2 t. salt
4 c. milk
16-oz. pkg. pasteurized process
    cheese spread, cubed

16-oz. pkg. elbow macaroni,
    cooked
paprika to taste

Melt butter in a saucepan over medium heat; stir in flour and salt.
Gradually add milk and stir until thickened. Add cheese, stirring until
melted. Combine macaroni and cheese sauce in a slow cooker;
sprinkle with paprika. Cover and cook on low setting for 4 hours.

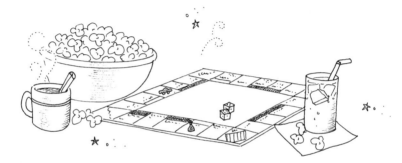

Start the week off right...make Monday night family night!
Play games, read stories...with dinner cooking away in the
slow cooker, there's plenty of time for fun!

Cheesy Parmesan Polenta

Serves 6

9 c. chicken broth
1/4 c. butter, sliced
1 bay leaf

3 c. instant polenta, uncooked
3 c. grated Parmesan cheese

In a saucepan over medium heat, bring broth, butter and bay leaf to a boil. Gradually whisk in polenta; add cheese and continue whisking until well blended. Transfer to a slow cooker. Cover and cook on low setting for 25 to 30 minutes. Discard bay leaf before serving.

Add rosy red color and spicy flavor to homemade applesauce...just stir in a spoonful of red cinnamon candies as it's cooking.

Chunky Applesauce

Makes 6 to 8 servings

10 apples, peeled, cored
    and cubed
1/2 c. water

3/4 c. sugar
Optional: 1 t. cinnamon

Combine all ingredients in a slow cooker; toss to mix. Cover and cook on low setting for 8 to 10 hours. Serve warm or keep refrigerated in a covered container.

Slow down and enjoy life.

-Eddie Cantor

Not Your Mother's Green Beans

28-oz. pkg. frozen cut green
   beans, thawed
1 onion, chopped
1 c. roasted red pepper strips,
   chopped

1/4 t. salt
1/8 t. pepper
10-oz. jar Alfredo sauce
2.8-oz. can French fried onions,
   divided

Combine all ingredients in a slow cooker, reserving half the French
fried onions. Cover and cook on high setting for 3 to 4 hours, stirring
after one hour. Just before serving, heat remaining French fried onions
in a small skillet over medium heat for 2 to 3 minutes, stirring
constantly. Stir casserole and sprinkle with fried onions.

The simplest table decorations are often the prettiest!
Try filling a basket with shiny red apples or fragrant
yellow lemons for the kitchen table.

Grandma's Corn

8-oz. pkg. cream cheese
1/4 c. butter
32-oz. pkg. frozen corn

1/3 c. sugar or sugar blend
  for baking
Optional: 1 to 3 T. water

Let cream cheese and butter soften in a slow cooker on low setting for about 10 minutes. Add corn and sugar or sugar substitute; stir well until corn is coated with cream cheese mixture. Cover and cook on low setting for 3 to 4 hours, stirring occasionally. If corn seems too thick, add water as needed just before serving.

When measuring sticky ingredients like honey or molasses,
spray the measuring cup with non-stick vegetable spray first.
The contents will slip right out and you'll get a more
accurate measurement.

Barbecue Molasses Beans

Serves 6 to 8

16-oz. pkg. dried pinto beans
3 c. water
1 onion, chopped

18-oz. bottle barbecue sauce
1/4 c. molasses
1/4 t. pepper

Combine all ingredients in a slow cooker; mix well. Cover and cook on low setting for 8 to 9 hours.

When time is short, a super-fast dessert is in order.
Fill sundae cups with cubes of angel food cake layered with
pie filling and topped with whipped cream...yummy!

Company Chicken & Stuffing

Serves 4

4 boneless, skinless chicken
    breasts
4 slices Swiss cheese
6-oz. pkg. chicken-flavored
    stuffing mix

2 10-3/4 oz. cans cream of
    chicken soup
1/2 c. chicken broth

Arrange chicken in slow cooker; top each piece with a slice of cheese.
Mix together stuffing mix, broth and soup; spoon into a slow cooker.
Cover and cook on low setting for 6 to 8 hours.

Don't worry about slow-cooker temperatures being below what's safe. The low setting is about 200 degrees, while high is about 300 degrees...both well above the safe temperature of 140 degrees.

Country Chicken & Dumplings   *Makes about 6 servings*

4 boneless, skinless chicken
   breasts
2 10-3/4 oz. cans cream of
   chicken soup

2 T. butter, sliced
1 onion, finely diced
2 10-oz. tubes refrigerated
   biscuits, torn

Place chicken, soup, butter and onion in a slow cooker; add enough water to cover. Cover and cook on high setting for 4 hours. Add biscuits to slow cooker; gently push biscuits into cooking liquid. Cover and continue cooking for about 1-1/2 hours, or until biscuits are done in the center.

dinner at 6pm tonight!

Pick up a package of refrigerated mashed potatoes at the grocery for a quick & easy side dish. Heat and stir in cream cheese, sour cream and butter to taste...as yummy as homemade.

Sour Cream Chicken

Makes 4 servings

4 boneless, skinless chicken
    breasts
16-oz. container sour cream

5-1/2 oz. pkg. baked chicken
    coating mix
mashed potatoes

Arrange chicken in a slow cooker. Mix together sour cream and
coating mix; spoon over chicken. Cover and cook on low setting for
4 to 5 hours. Serve chicken over mashed potatoes.

If it's time to buy a new slow cooker, look for one with
a removable crock...they're so much easier to clean!

No-Fuss Turkey Breast

Makes 6 servings

5-lb. turkey breast
1.35-oz. pkg. onion soup mix

16-oz. can whole-berry
cranberry sauce

Place turkey breast in a slow cooker. Combine soup mix and cranberry sauce; spread over turkey. Cover and cook on low setting for 6 to 8 hours.

An instant appetizer...set out a warm loaf of Italian bread
and a little dish of olive oil sprinkled with Italian
seasoning for dipping.

Mom's Chicken Italiano

Serves 4 to 6

2 to 3 lbs. boneless, skinless
   chicken breasts
2 10-3/4 oz. cans golden
   mushroom soup

2 14-1/2 oz. cans diced
   tomatoes
1 c. onion, chopped
1 t. dried basil

Arrange chicken in a slow cooker. Mix together remaining ingredients and pour over chicken. Cover and cook on low setting for 8 hours. Cut or shred chicken into bite-size pieces before serving.

Not able to use chicken within two days of purchasing?
No problem! Properly packaged, chicken can be frozen and
will maintain top quality for up to one year.

Charlene's Ritzy Chicken

Serves 4 to 6

10-3/4 oz. can cream of
   chicken soup
1 pt. sour cream
1 sleeve round buttery
   crackers, crushed

1/2 c. butter, melted
4 to 6 boneless, skinless
   chicken breasts
mashed potatoes

Combine soup and sour cream in a small bowl; set aside. In a separate bowl, mix together crackers and butter. Place chicken in a slow cooker; spoon soup mixture over top and sprinkle with cracker mixture. Cover and cook on low setting for 7 to 9 hours, or on high setting for 4 to 5 hours. Serve over mashed potatoes.

Freezing cooked rice makes for quick-fix meals later. Use it for stir-fry dishes or mix in fresh vegetables for an easy side dish...just freeze servings in flat plastic zipping bags.

Pineapple Chicken

Serves 4 to 6

3 to 4 lbs. boneless, skinless
    chicken
16-oz. bottle Catalina salad
    dressing

20-oz. can pineapple chunks,
    drained and 1/4 cup juice
    reserved

Place chicken in slow cooker. Add salad dressing, pineapple and
reserved juice. Cover and cook on low setting for 8 to 10 hours, or
on high setting for 6 hours.

Keep fast-cooking ramen noodles on hand for quick meals.
Simply top drained noodles with gravy for a speedy,
yummy side dish!

Easy Slow-Cooker Steak

Makes 5 servings

2 to 2-1/2 lb. beef round steak,
    cut into serving-size pieces
1-1/2 oz. pkg. onion soup mix

1/4 c. water
10-3/4 oz. can cream of
    mushroom soup

Place beef in a slow cooker. Add soup mix, water and soup. Cover and cook on low setting for 6 to 8 hours.

It's best to thaw meat before slow cooking, if possible.
Otherwise, cook on high for the first hour, then reduce
to low and cook as usual.

Sandra's Slow-Cooker Brisket

Makes 6 servings

1 onion, sliced
3 to 4-lb. beef brisket
1 T. smoke-flavored
  cooking sauce

12-oz. bottle chili sauce
salt and pepper to taste

Arrange onion slices in a slow cooker; place brisket on top of onion.
Add smoke-flavored cooking sauce; pour chili sauce over brisket.
Sprinkle with salt and pepper. Cover and cook on low setting for
10 to 12 hours.

All-day slow cooking works wonders on inexpensive, less-tender cuts of beef...arm and chuck roast, rump roast, round steak and stew beef cook up juicy and delicious.

Baja Steak

Serves 6

1-1/2 lbs. boneless beef round steak, cut into serving-size pieces
2 c. frozen corn, thawed and drained
18-oz. jar chunky garden salsa
15-oz. can black beans, drained and rinsed
1 onion, chopped
1/2 c. water
1/2 t. salt
Optional: 1/8 t. red pepper flakes

Place beef in a slow cooker. Mix remaining ingredients together; pour over beef. Cover and cook on low setting for 8 to 9 hours.

Cook egg noodles the easy way, no watching needed.
Bring water to a rolling boil, then turn off heat. Add noodles
and let stand for 20 minutes, stirring twice.

Slow-Cooker Beef Stroganoff

Serves 4

1 lb. beef round steak, cubed
2 1.35-oz. pkgs. beefy onion
  soup mix
10-3/4 oz. can cream of
  celery soup
10-3/4 oz. can cream of
  mushroom soup
Optional: 1/2 c. sour cream
cooked egg noodles or rice

Place beef, soup mix and soups in a slow cooker. Cover and cook on low setting for 6 to 8 hours, stirring occasionally. Just before serving, stir in sour cream, if using. Serve over cooked noodles or rice.

Lit candles are a quick way to add warmth and charm to
a table setting. Make the most of their soft glow
by setting candles on mirrors.

Oh-So-Easy Lasagna

Serves 8

1 to 2 lbs. ground beef, browned
    and drained
26-oz. jar Parmesan & Romano
    pasta sauce

8-oz. pkg. bowtie pasta, cooked
12-oz. container cottage cheese
16-oz. pkg. shredded mozzarella
    cheese

Mix together ground beef and pasta sauce. In a slow cooker, layer
half each of ground beef mixture, pasta, cottage cheese and shredded
cheese. Repeat with remaining ingredients. Cover and cook on low
setting for 6 to 8 hours, or on high setting for 3 to 4 hours.

If a recipe calls for stewed tomatoes, take advantage of Mexican or Italian-style. They already have the seasonings added, so there are fewer ingredients for you to buy and measure!

1-2-3 Tomato-Onion Roast

Serves 6 to 8

3 to 4-lb. beef chuck roast   14-1/2 oz. can stewed tomatoes
1.35-oz. pkg. onion soup mix

Place roast in a slow cooker; top with soup mix and tomatoes. Cover and cook on low setting for 8 hours.

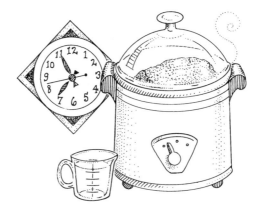

Slow cookers are super year 'round...no matter what the occasion. So grab a friend and head out to the local craft show or farmers' market. When you come home, a delicious meal will be waiting for you!

Smoky Hobo Dinner

Serves 6

5 potatoes, peeled and quartered
1 head cabbage, coarsely
    chopped
16-oz. pkg. baby carrots
1 onion, thickly sliced

salt and pepper to taste
14-oz. pkg. smoked pork
    sausage, sliced into
    2-inch pieces
1/2 c. water

Spray a slow cooker with non-stick vegetable spray. Layer vegetables, sprinkling each layer with salt and pepper. Place sausage on top. Pour water down one side of slow cooker. Cover and cook on low setting for 6 to 8 hours.

A tasty apple coleslaw goes well with pork. Simply toss together
a large bag of coleslaw mix, a chopped Granny Smith apple
and one cup of mayonnaise.

Homestyle Pork Chops

Makes 6 servings

1/2 c. all-purpose flour
1-1/2 t. dry mustard
1/2 t. salt
1/2 t. garlic powder

6 pork chops
2 T. oil
10-1/2 oz. can chicken broth

Combine flour, mustard, salt and garlic powder in a shallow bowl.
Coat pork chops in mixture; set aside any remaining mixture. In a
skillet, brown pork chops in oil; drain. Stir together broth and
remaining flour mixture in a slow cooker; add pork chops. Cover
and cook on high setting for 2-1/2 hours.

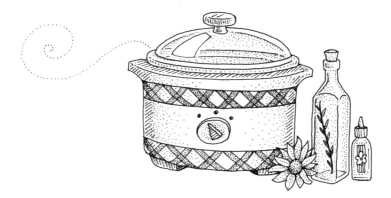

Stock up at supermarket sales on large packages of
ground beef, chicken or pork chops, then repackage into
recipe-size portions before freezing.

This & That Pork Chops

Makes 4 servings

4 pork chops
1/2 t. salt
1/4 t. pepper
1 onion, sliced 1/4-inch thick

1 lemon, sliced 1/4-inch thick
1/4 c. brown sugar, packed
1/4 c. catsup

Place pork chops in a slow cooker; sprinkle with salt and pepper. Top with onion and lemon. Sprinkle with brown sugar; drizzle with catsup. Cover and cook on low setting for 6 hours.

Keep side dishes simple...boil new potatoes just until tender,
then gently toss with butter and parsley. Quick & easy!

Oktoberfest Pork Roast

Serves 4 to 6

3 to 4-lb. boneless pork roast
salt and pepper to taste
1 T. shortening
2 apples, peeled, cored and
    quartered

32-oz. pkg. sauerkraut
1 c. apple juice or water
Optional: 17-oz. pkg. fresh or
    frozen pierogies

Sprinkle roast with salt and pepper. Melt shortening in a skillet over high heat; brown roast on all sides. Place roast in a slow cooker. Add apples, sauerkraut and juice or water; blend. Add pierogies, if using; push down gently to partially submerge them in the liquid. Cover and cook on low setting for 8 to 9 hours.

A rainy day cure-all...toss together ingredients for a tasty slower-cooker meal, make some popcorn and enjoy a family movie marathon. When you're ready for dinner, it's ready for you!

No-Peek Shepherd's Pie

Makes 6 servings

1 lb. ground pork sausage,
  browned and drained
10-oz. pkg. frozen peas
  and carrots

24-oz. pkg. prepared mashed
  potatoes
12-oz. jar beef gravy

Combine sausage with peas and carrots in a slow cooker. Spoon
mashed potatoes evenly over mixture; top with gravy. Do not stir.
Cover and cook on low setting for 4 to 6 hours.

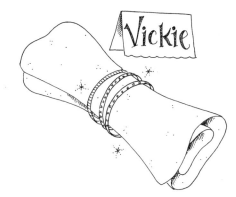

Vintage-style souvenir tea towels make whimsical oversized napkins...handy for messy-but-tasty foods like barbecued ribs, corn on the cob and watermelon!

Country-Style Ribs

Serves 4 to 6

2 lbs. boneless country-style
  pork ribs, cut into
  serving-size pieces
1 onion, sliced

3 cloves garlic, minced
2/3 c. barbecue sauce
1/3 c. apple jelly

Place ribs, onion and garlic in a slow cooker that has been sprayed with non-stick vegetable spray. Cover and cook on low setting for 8 to 10 hours. Drain; discard juices. In a small bowl, combine barbecue sauce and jelly; spread evenly over ribs. Cover and cook on high setting for an additional 25 minutes, or until ribs are glazed.

Write it on your heart that every day is
the best day of the year.

-Ralph Waldo Emerson

Party Cola Ham

Makes 8 to 12 servings

3 to 4-lb. fully-cooked ham
1/2 c. brown sugar, packed

1 t. dry mustard
1/2 c. cola, divided

Cut a shallow diamond pattern in the surface of ham and set aside.
Combine brown sugar and mustard; add enough cola to make a paste.
Rub mixture over ham and place in slow cooker. Pour in remaining
cola; cover and cook on high setting for one hour. Reduce to low
setting and cook for 6 to 7 hours.

For a quick dessert garnish, chop and toast nuts in a shallow
baking pan at 350 degrees for 5 to 10 minutes. Cool, then
place in plastic bags and freeze. Ready to sprinkle
on desserts when you need them.

Upside-Down Blueberry Cake

Serves 10 to 12

21-oz. can blueberry pie filling
2 egg whites
18-1/4 oz. pkg. lemon cake mix

1 c. water
1/3 c. applesauce

Spread pie filling in a slow cooker that has been sprayed with non-stick vegetable spray. With an electric mixer on high speed, beat egg whites until soft peaks form, about 2 minutes. Stir in remaining ingredients just until combined. Pour over filling; do not stir. Place 8 paper towels on top of slow cooker to absorb moisture. Cover and cook on high setting for 2 hours, or until a toothpick tests clean when inserted near center. Remove crock from slow cooker; remove lid and paper towels. Cool cake for 15 minutes. Place a large serving plate over crock; carefully invert onto plate.

Freeze whipped cream to use later...what a time-saver!
Drop tablespoonfuls onto a chilled baking sheet and freeze.
Remove and store in a plastic zipping bag. Serve on
dessert portions...whipped cream will thaw in minutes.

Peachy Dump Cake

Makes 6 to 8 servings

2 14-1/2 oz. cans peach
   pie filling
1 t. lemon juice
18-1/2 oz. pkg. yellow cake mix

1/2 c. chopped pecans
1/2 c. butter, melted
Garnish: whipped cream or
   vanilla ice cream

Pour pie filling into a slow cooker that has been sprayed with
non-stick vegetable spray. Drizzle with lemon juice. In a separate
bowl, combine dry cake mix, pecans and melted butter. Spread over
pie filling. Cover and cook on low setting for 4 hours, or on high
setting for 2 hours. Serve with whipped cream or ice cream.

Bread pudding is a wonderful way to use up leftover bread. Try French bread or extra muffins for an extra-tasty dessert!

Cozy Apple Bread Pudding

Serves 6

8 to 9 slices cinnamon-raisin
    bread, cubed
3 eggs, beaten
2 c. milk

1/2 c. sugar
21-oz. can apple pie filling
Optional: whipped cream or
    ice cream

Spread bread cubes in a single layer on an ungreased baking sheet.
Bake at 300 degrees for 10 to 15 minutes until dry, stirring twice.
Cool. In a large bowl, whisk eggs, milk and sugar. Gently stir in pie
filling and bread cubes. Pour into a slow cooker that has been sprayed
with non-stick vegetable spray. Cover and cook on low setting for
3 hours, or until puffy and a knife inserted near the center comes out
clean. Uncover and let stand for 30 to 45 minutes; pudding will fall
as it cools. Spoon into dessert dishes; garnish as desired.

Try these easy dessert topping ideas...gummy fruit candy, whipped topping, conversation hearts, mini chocolate chips, sprinkles or a drizzle of chocolate syrup. Sweet and simple.

Unbelievable Caramel Pie

Makes 6 to 8 servings

2 14-oz. cans sweetened
   condensed milk
9-inch graham cracker crust

Garnish: whipped topping, mini
   semi-sweet chocolate chips

Pour condensed milk into a slow cooker that has been sprayed with non-stick vegetable spray. Cover and cook on low setting for 3-1/2 to 4 hours. After 2-1/2 hours, milk will begin to thicken; begin stirring every 15 minutes. When thick and golden, stir again until smooth; pour into crust and chill. Garnish with whipped topping and chocolate chips.

Take along a dessert in a slow cooker to a party or
meeting...simply wrap it in a towel to keep it warm. Serve
within an hour or plug it in at a low setting.

Easy-Peasy Berry Cobbler

Makes 8 to 12 servings

16-oz. pkg. frozen mixed
    berries
1/2 c. sugar

12-oz. tube refrigerated biscuits
cinnamon to taste

Pour frozen berries into a slow cooker and stir in sugar. Arrange
biscuits on top; sprinkle with cinnamon to taste. Cover and cook on
high setting for 3 hours. Serve warm.

To speed banana ripening, place them in a plastic bag.
To help them stay fresh longer, refrigerate them. The peels
will darken, but the bananas will last for about 2 weeks.

Bananas Foster

1/2 c. butter, melted
1/4 c. brown sugar, packed
6 bananas, cut into 1-inch slices

1/4 c. rum or 1/4 t. rum extract
Garnish: vanilla ice cream

Stir together butter, brown sugar, bananas and rum or extract in a
slow cooker. Cover and cook on low setting for one hour. To serve,
spoon over scoops of ice cream.

Purchasing a new slow cooker? Look for one that has a
"warm" setting...it's perfect for keeping dips toasty
throughout potlucks and parties.

Rogene's Homestyle Custard

Serves 4 to 6

2 c. milk
5 eggs, beaten
1/3 c. super-fine sugar

1 t. vanilla extract
1/8 t. salt
1/4 t. nutmeg

Mix together all ingredients except nutmeg in a large bowl; pour into a slow cooker. Sprinkle nutmeg over top. Cover and cook on low setting for 8 hours.

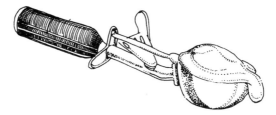

Dollop fresh whipped cream on warm slow-cooker desserts...
irresistible! Pour a pint of whipping cream into a deep,
narrow bowl. Beat with an electric mixer on medium speed,
gradually increasing to high speed. When soft peaks form,
add sugar to taste.

Chocolate Concoction

Makes 8 to 10 servings

18-1/4 oz. pkg. devil's food
    cake mix
16-oz. container sour cream
3.9-oz. pkg. instant chocolate
    pudding mix
1-1/2 c. semi-sweet
    chocolate chips

4 eggs, beaten
1 c. water
Optional: French vanilla
    ice cream

Beat together all ingredients except ice cream until smooth. Pour into a slow cooker that has been sprayed with non-stick vegetable spray. Cover and cook on low setting for 6 to 8 hours. Serve with ice cream, if desired.

A chocolate lover's delight! Fill a mini slow cooker with
chips or chunks of chocolate and heat on low until melted.
Stir, then dip in strawberries, cookies, or drizzle
over your favorite cake or brownies.

Hot Fudge Brownies

Serves 8

20-oz. pkg. brownie mix
1 c. chocolate syrup
1 c. hot water

Optional: vanilla ice cream,
    whipped topping

Prepare brownie mix according to package instructions. Spray a slow cooker with non-stick vegetable spray. Spread brownie batter evenly into a slow cooker. Mix together syrup and hot water; pour evenly over brownie batter. Cover and cook on high setting for 2-1/2 to 3 hours, until edges are set. Remove lid; let stand for 30 minutes, or until set. Spoon onto serving plates. Serve with ice cream or whipped topping, if desired.

Let your slow cooker be your party helper, keeping meatballs or chicken wings warm and cheesy dips hot and bubbly!

You're Invited!
To a Slow-Cooker Potluck

Theme: ....
Date: ....
Host: ....
Address: ....

Phone: ....
Email: ....
Please bring: ....
....

© Gooseberry Patch

Copy, Color & Cut Out!

INDEX

INDEX

Our Story

Back in 1984, we were next-door neighbors raising our families in the little town of Delaware, Ohio. Two moms with small children, we were looking for a way to do what we loved and stay home with the kids too. We had always shared a love of home cooking and making memories with family & friends and so, after many a conversation over the backyard fence, **Gooseberry Patch** was born.

We put together our first catalog at our kitchen tables, enlisting the help of our loved ones wherever we could. From that very first mailing, we found an immediate connection with many of our customers and it wasn't long before we began receiving letters, photos and recipes from these new friends. In 1992, we put together our very first cookbook, compiled from hundreds of these recipes and, the rest, as they say, is history.

Hard to believe it's been almost 40 years since those kitchen-table days! From that original little **Gooseberry Patch** family, we've grown to include an amazing group of creative folks who love cooking, decorating and creating as much as we do. Today, we're best known for our homestyle, family-friendly cookbooks, now recognized as national bestsellers.

One thing's for sure, we couldn't have done it without our friends all across the country. Each year, we're honored to turn thousands of your recipes into our collectible cookbooks. Our hope is that each book captures the stories and heart of all of you who have shared with us. Whether you've been with us since the beginning or are just discovering us, welcome to the **Gooseberry Patch** family!

Visit our website anytime
www.gooseberrypatch.com

Jo Ann & Vickie

1·800·854·6673